A Career in AVIATION

JERRY A. BURTON

Copyright © 2023 by Jerry A. Burton.

All rights reserved. No part of this book may be reproduced, stored, or transmitted by any means—whether auditory, graphic, mechanical, or electronic—without written permission of both publisher and author, except in the case of brief excerpts used in critical articles and reviews. Unauthorized reproduction of any part of this work is illegal and is punishable by law.

Library of Congress Control Number: 2016906787

ISBN: 979-8-89031-423-9 (sc)
ISBN: 979-8-89031-424-6 (hc)
ISBN: 979-8-89031-425-3 (e)

Because of the dynamic nature of the Internet, any web addresses or links contained in this book may have changed since publication and may no longer be valid. The views expressed in this work are solely those of the author and do not necessarily reflect the views of the publisher, and the publisher hereby disclaims any responsibility for them.

THE EWINGS PUBLISHING

One Galleria Blvd., Suite 1900, Metairie, LA 70001
(504) 702-6708

FOREWORD

Dedicated to my deceased father and mother,
Harold and Gertrude Burton.

In this book, you will find the life story of one army aviator from high school to retirement. It begins with a young Iowa farm boy searching for a career and finding a lifelong association with the US Army Aviation Branch.

I had the opportunity to get into the farming business with my father, but finding all the hard work that was involved, I decided to enlist in the army and attend the flight training program and pursue a career in aviation.

This life story begins with enlistment, basic training, flight school, and a life in the flying world. It covers two deployments to Vietnam, each one year in length, a segment with the Iowa and Alabama Army National Guard, and sixteen years stationed at the home of Army Aviation: Fort Rucker, Alabama. I was a ground and flight simulator instructor for a civilian contractor, FlightSafety International, following my retirement from the military. I also worked with a FAR Part 135 charter company in Iowa. With that company, I flew a Piper Aztec and Navajo and a Cessna 182, 210, 340, 402, and 414. I also flew a Skymaster part-time. I was assigned duties as chief pilot for them.

My last assignment was with SIMCOM training centers in Scottsdale, Arizona; Miami, Florida; and Orlando, Florida. While I worked with them, I had duties of ground, flight simulator, and aircraft flight instructor. I was also selected as assistant training center manager, ultimately ending my career as the director of business jet training in Miami, Florida. SIMCOM was a FAR Part 142 training center. After leaving them in 2002, I moved to Iowa for a life of retired living.

Some of the photos have dates of 2015 on them; this is when I made copies of the originals. All the dates, places, and facts are accurate to the best of my memory.

AIRPLANES AND HELICOPTERS I HAVE FLOWN

Piper: 140, 180, 235, Twin Comanche, Aztec, Navajo, Malibu, and Seneca.

Cessna: 120, 150, 170, 172, 180, 182, 210, 340, 402, and 414.

Beech: Baron, King Air 90a, c, g, Duke, and King Air 200.

Hiller helicopters: OH-23B, OH-23D.

Hughes helicopters: TH-55, OH-6A, and Hughes 500.

Brantly: B2B

Bell: TH-13, H-13, OH-58A, UH-1A, UH-1B, UH-1C, UH-1D, UH-1H, and UH1-M.

US Army: T-41, T-42, O-1, U-1, and U-6.

Lear Jet: Lear Jet 23

CERTIFICATES AND RATINGS

I was certified by the FAA and hold the following certificates:

- Airline Transport Pilot airplane single and multi-engine land and rotocraft helicopter with type ratings in the Lear Jet and Bell 206.

- A Flight Instructor certificate with rotorcraft/helicopter, airplane (single and multi-engine), instrument, rotorcraft/helicopter, and airplane.

- A Ground Instructor certificate and an expired designated pilot examiner certificate.

I graduated from high school as an underachiever in 1963. Just happy to have my diploma, I did not want to go to work right away, so I took off to Wyoming to visit a high school classmate. I spent two months with his family in the town of Lusk, Wyoming.

From Wyoming, I visited a cousin in Bartlesville, Oklahoma. He worked for Phillips Petroleum Company. I went to work for Phillips soon after, as I soon found out it was necessary to pay the bills. I worked a few months there and then transferred within the company to an oil exploration team in North Dakota. The team chief was a pilot, and he soon got me interested in flying. The work was physically hard, but I liked it. I saved my wages until I had enough to start my flying career.

I began flying a Cessna 120 from Dickinson, North Dakota, and soloed. Next came the cross-country into Bismarck, North Dakota, with my team chief in the backseat of a Cessna 172, observing my skills. All went well with civilian flying, but I ran out of money before I could get my pilot certificate.

Flying was very enjoyable for me, so I started looking around in the aviation career fields. Since I was 1-A in the draft program, I elected to enlist into the flight training program with the United States Army.

I quit my job with Phillips and said, "Take me, I am yours." So the recruiter sent me by train from Casper, Wyoming, to Denver, Colorado, for testing and my enlistment physical. I passed the mental and physical tests with flying colors.

I signed on the dotted line, and off I went. The army gave me thirty days before I was to report for duty. I was able to visit with friends and family in Iowa before reporting to Fort Des Moines to be sworn into the US Army.

On the fifth of October 1965, I took my oath of office. One other recruit and myself were picked to be in charge of the busload of recruits as we traveled by bus to Fort Leonard, Missouri (they called it "Fort lost in the woods"). I later became best friends with that recruit and remain that way today. We arrived at the military base later that day.

B asic training was physical, mental, and combat training. I excelled at running the mile and on the firing range. I was a member of the 400 club for fitness and rated expert on the firing range.

Basic training came and went, and then it was off to Fort Wolters, Texas, for the first phase of flight training. The first part was warrant officer training. This was shaping us into warrant officer material, before the entry to the flight line and learning to fly helicopters.

The first day on the flight line was a scary one; trying to hover the thing was a monumental task. It was described as trying to stand on a basketball without falling off. Many flight hours were spent between the ground and ten feet in the air. But as with everything else, hovering was mastered. Then came the flight maneuvers, a lot of them—takeoff to a hover, normal takeoff, normal landing (sometimes not so normal), takeoff over an obstacle and steep approach, along with upper air work- climbs, descents, turns, and talking on the radios. They were all exciting things and kept me busy.

The first day that we were given permission to fly without the flight instructor (called flying solo) was very exciting. We were allowed to make three takeoffs and three landings, then back with the flight instructor. Another exciting thing about your first solo was the fact that the rest of your class got to throw you into the swimming pool with your flight suit on.

As we advanced in flight training, we practiced more and more difficult flight maneuvers like autorotations, which are landing on the runway without the use of the engine, and confined area operations, where we landed into designated small landing areas off the base. At first, we had to land then secure the helicopter, leaving the engine running, and conduct a recon of the landing zone. We then laid out rocks to indicate the takeoff path then got back into the helicopter and made a confined area departure. We later conducted the Landing Zone (LZ) reconnaissance from the inside of the helicopters.

The flight training at Fort Wolters was called primary, and then we moved to Fort Rucker, Alabama, for advanced flight training. We got checked out in the UH-1 helicopters. We learned most of the previous maneuvers along with a bunch more.

Upon completing flight training at Fort Rucker, each class conducted a multi-helicopter formation flight over the main parade field on the post. It was quite a sight—seems like there were ten to twelve flights of three Huey helicopters, all in formation. Formation meant that two or more helicopters were in the air at one time, going in the same direction, and being very close to each other.

We wore starched fatigues during primary and advanced flight training. When we graduated from Fort Rucker, most of us went directly to Vietnam on our first assignment. We were issued jungle fatigues and packed our duffel bags, and off we went.

I was a little scared as we flew across the pond to Vietnam, and I was convinced that I would not be coming home. I wrote that in my diary and kept it up-to-date that first year I was in Republic of Vietnam. It took the Ninety-Second Replacement Battalion two weeks to decide where they wanted to send me. So I hopped a flight to Vung Tau and visited Jim DeGrief, a very close friend I had gone through basic training with. I had a nice visit with him at his base there and then went back to Saigon to be reassigned.

I was assigned to the Fifty-Second Aviation Battalion, 155th Assault Helicopter Company in Buon Me Thuot, RVN. I got there in mid-March of 1967 and went right to flying. Our first sergeant required us to write a letter back home, just in case we did not make it home. He put these letters in the safe and told us we could get them back when we went home. Life in RVN went very fast, and we worked all seven days of the week—the enemy did not rest on the weekend. I flew between 100 to 140 flying hours a month. The first six months, I flew the troop- carrying Hueys, and the last six months, I flew with the gunships. The gunships were more fun as you didn't have to land in the landing zones; you just flew around, giving cover to the slicks that were landing so they didn't get shot down. That was a thing that I had a hard time dealing with, seeing the enemy get killed by my hand. It never got easier; you just didn't throw up as much. Got lots of memories of those days, but I try not to talk about them too much as they give me a hard time sleeping at night. The VA diagnosed me with PTSD later in life, but it was caused by those days in RVN. I've seen and did a lot of really nasty things over there, most too ugly to tell. One time, the South Vietnam army officers took us to an old barn where they proudly showed off an eight-foot pile of last week's dead bad-guy soldiers' bodies. Not good for the ole brain. I remain on medication today and probably will for life. I am a regular visitor at the VA hospital. I am including some of my diary entries so you will have an idea what it was like day after day.

I want you to know that on April 4 of 1967, I surrendered my life to Christ, as I knew I could not make it without him as my copilot. I had peace and calm that came about me after that day that allowed me to come out of several bad situations with only bumps and bruises. He was always with me throughout my flying career, always protecting me—I praise God for that amazing relationship.

TOUR IN VIETNAM

2015/09/13

My first tour started in RVN in 1967, and the second started in 1970. The dates of some of the photos are when I transferred them into this format.

This is a group of mountain yard families that were being relocated to a resettlement area near Pleiku. These folks were good people. They were being troubled by the Vietcong, who were stealing their food and the feed for their animals. The United States relocated them for their own safety.

It's me walking around the mountain yard village.
They were very poor people with little to wear.

This was a mountain yard house complete with a wooden deck for sunning themselves. Note the corn growing in the background. I am also wearing my "chicken plate" (slang for bulletproof vest).

Here we are inside that house, looking at some of the storage containers for their food. Most of the houses were made of bamboo and straw.

This view shows a mountain yard "happy house," or place to go and have a drink of rice wine—a very crude drink, but it was all they had available. Tried it; didn't like it.

This was one of the resettlement areas that the Vietnam people were brought to after their villages were overrun or destroyed. Uncle Sam likely paid for these. This one was in II Corps near the town of Pleiku.

A bunker where we went when there was an enemy attack. Been there several times.

Looking east down the main street of our compound.
Buildings all surrounded with sandbags.

The Officers' Club. Spent many a night inside this place.

The officers' mess hall, where we ate our meals when we were not out flying.

Our clothes-washing machine: two Vietnamese ladies that did them by hand. Only paid them two dollars a week, and they polished our shoes also.

Standing next to our bunker where we all gathered
when we were attacked by the enemy.

Our outside restroom. It was right next to the pistol firing range—you got startled every once in a while. At that period, there were no females at our compound.

An aerial view of our compound and airfield looking to the east. We were located in II Corps next to a small town called Buon Me Thuot. The airstrip can be seen on the far right of the photo.

One of our troop-carrying helicopters that was badly damaged by a mortar round the night before. Note the hole in the ground just right and aft of the landing gear.

Me in my jungle fatigues, holding an unexploded mortar round that landed just outside my hooch (where I was sleeping).

The local food market. What did not get sold that day went on the ground in the street. In the morning, it was okay; but by midafternoon, it smelled terrible. Looked bad also.

A small lake in the highlands of II Corps area. There were a couple boats the army had that some troops went waterskiing behind. But you frequently got shot at, so I never exposed myself to hostile fire unless it was a mission requirement.

These were the boats they used to ski with. I was happy about something but really don't know why. You can see in the background it had been raining, and it was likely cool outside.

I'm resting my hand on the M60 machine gun attached to the helicopter—had one on each side of the helicopter.

I flew this one; the gunner operated the machine gun.

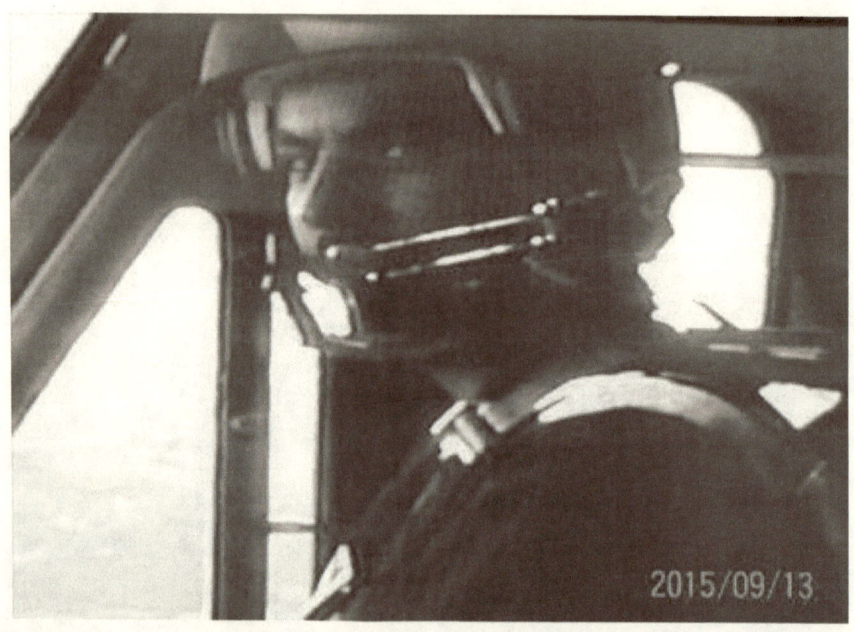

I was flying right seat this day; we were up above some clouds.

These were salt paddies. They would allow seawater in and let the sun dry it out so they could harvest the salt. This was very near the coast of Vietnam.

My office, made from an old ammunition box. Rather crude, but remember where I was. The door folded up and had a lock on it. We lived in tents surrounded by sandbags.

I had been in the country a while here as the stache was pretty grown out.

Everyone owned and wore a big watch over there;
they were real cheap at the exchange.

These round boats were what the natives used to fish from. Note the sandy beach. Don't know how they kept the water out; it didn't look like something I would get in.

The South China Sea looking from the beach eastward at an offshore island. The water was very clear, and there were lots of small fishing boats.

Nha Trang, a city by the South China Sea.
Airfield in center of the photo.

This day, I was flying a gunship. Note the rockets mounted on the side of the helicopter.

I was thinking about the day's mission, and somebody caught me in the thinking mode.

Young children would always crowd around
to get anything we had to give.

Four of the gunship pilots contemplating the next mission. I am on the far left.

Lady with the hat on is serving a meal at noon. A mobile café, if you will.

The city of Da Lat, known for its fresh veggies and RVN military academy. Many missions there. The valleys outside town were filled with fields of fresh veggies. We had some sent to our base—one of the very few fresh foods we had to eat.

The golf course at Da Lat, for the Vietnam officers.
I never played there, just flew over it.

The veggie farms I was telling you about, very well taken care of.

An RVN remote outpost. The soldiers had their families live right there with them. We took some officials to this outpost for a visit.

Here, an older child takes care of a baby brother
at the outpost in the background.

A Vietnamese soldier at his post, overlooking
the low ground for spotting the enemy.

Part of my unit waiting to insert RVN troops into an LZ (landing zone). We always took at least two gunships along on a mission—more if the situation indicated a chance of a lot of bad guys.

A look from the other end of the lineup. We would insert the troops then wait and bring them back late in the day.

I am standing outside the tactical operations center, waiting to attend a briefing for the next day. This mission was up in Northern Vietnam, flying out of Ka San and west across the border.

I am practicing rappelling down this man-made tower with the help of Special Forces guys.

The air force parachuting supplies to a US outpost.
Likely the only way we could get supplies.

Two enemy troops being questioned while over the South China Sea. Only one returned to land. That one did a lot of talking after his comrade went for a swim.

Looking southeast over the South China Sea, waiting for a passenger to return. Note the big thunderstorm in upper right background and the island offshore. Water was blue and pretty.

This helicopter was resupplying a unit based near this town. I do not remember the name of the town though. You can see the sea in the upper background. I am looking easterly.

Flying low-level over some populated area. Usually, we were either real low-flying or up really high so we did not get shot down.

Wreckage of one of our helicopters that crash-landed into the trees; no one was hurt bad though.

A bad accident where two of my friends were killed. Mechanical problems brought this one down. It was close to our base camp.

In the right center is the helicopter I was in when we landed short of the LZ and rolled down the hill. The troops flew out, and some were killed, but the crew of four just had bumps and bangs. Captain Pullum was leading this flight; we were the last one in and landed short on the side of the hill. Only time I crashed. The other pilot was flying—I was just along for the ride.

A CH-47 and two Hueys were picking up the pieces from the crash. Our crashed helicopter is in the left center—hard to see. I got out through the overhead green window as we stopped lying on the left side, and I was on the right side.

Again, we are in the left upper center. (Sounds weird, huh? But that's where we were.) Did not break the skin, so no Purple Heart. That's one medal I did not want to receive.

CWO Brad Jones and me in Bangkok, Thailand.
Brad, on the left, and I visited this Buddhist temple.
We were on a rest and recuperation trip from RVN.

Me on the left at the steps of the same building.
Note the camera in my right hand.

I am standing in front of the hotel I stayed at on my second R & R in Taipei, Taiwan.

Brad and I having breakfast on our last day
before returning to Vietnam.

The business district in Taiwan: small and
lots of businesses in one place.

And that was my first tour of duty in RVN. Upon returning to the United States, I was assigned to Hunter Army Airfield, Georgia. I was a flight and ground instructor for the instructor pilots that went there to teach basic flight training. I did that for about a year and then the commander moved me to be the battalion aviation safety officer. I received a promotion from chief warrant officer (W2) to first lieutenant (forgot to mention that after my initial flight training, I was commissioned as a chief warrant officer [W1] then received a promotion to W2 while in RVN). I spent less than a year at that new assignment. While I was at Hunter, I took training in airplanes and received a dual rating in fixed-wing airplanes for the army.

Then came the time to return to RVN for a second tour. I went to a transition course at Fort Rucker for OH-6A helicopters and a gunnery course for mini-gun training on the same helicopter. Then a little vacation at home and across the big pond, as it was referred to back then. Was on orders to be assigned to the NET (new equipment training) team in Vung Tau, but when I got in the country, they might use my skills in a different area. I was sent to the Seventh of the First Air Cavalry as a standardization officer (that's watching over the unit's pilot training programs and doing flight standardization check rides). I was on the squadron staff and was required to give reports every week on the status of the squadron training program.

While on my second tour, I obtained two war trophies. One was an old Mauser that had been used as a sniper rifle by the bad guys. The second one was a new, never-fired SKS rifle that had been obtained in a weapons raid across the border. I had several pilots in the unit looking out for me and was lucky to get them. I registered them in RVN and was able to carry them back to the United States in my baggage. Just a couple years ago, I donated them to the Gold Star Museum at the headquarters of the Iowa National Guard in Des Moines, Iowa. The new one is on display there today.

I did not take as many pictures on the second trip but have placed a few of them for your viewing pleasure.

Dad's farm home that I grew up on—about
seven miles southwest of Alden, Iowa.

My best friend standing at attention in honor of my return from RVN.

My closest friend then and now, Jim DeGrief. We went to basic training at Fort Leonard Wood, Missouri, and later met up in RVN. Great man—lots of interesting times together, both good and bad.

Last tour in RVN, I got the opportunity to visit my uncle Arthur Stout's memorial in Manila, Philippines. Caught a flight to Clark Air Force Base.

This was my home while on second tour and stationed at Vinh Long. I was assigned to HHT 7 / 1 Air Cavalry and was the chief instructor pilot (standardization officer).

This was my office, a lean-to with no doors.
But it got the rain off my head.

This was a steak BBQ between the buildings.
That was good beef, but not like Iowa beef.

This was a hotel I stayed at while visiting Arthur's memorial.

This is the memorial where Arthur Stout's name appears.
Each one of those walls is full of names of the military.

Taxicab in Manila—lots of them, brightly colored.

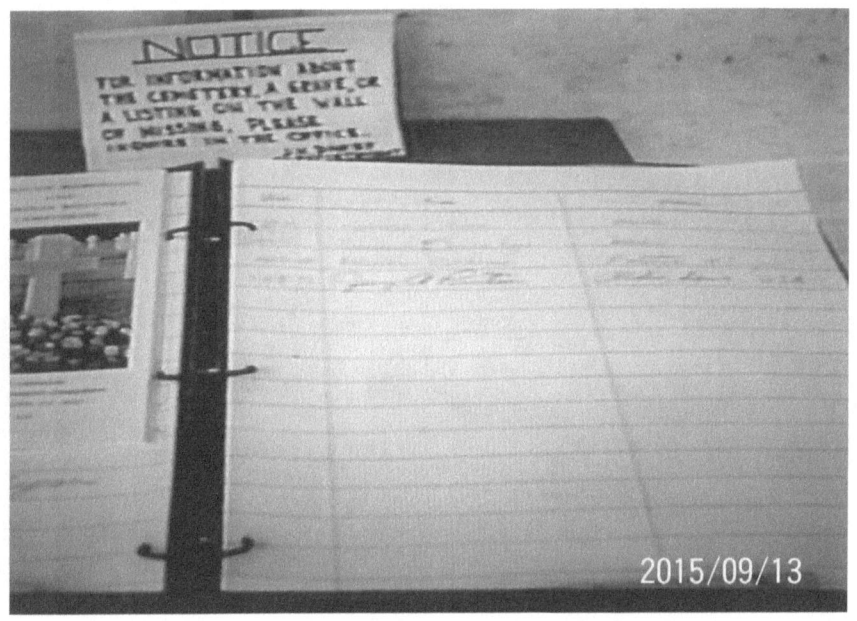

Book that I signed my name in at the memorial.

I left this plaque at the office of the memorial,
from the Stout family.

Standing in front of the chapel at the memorial, holding the plaque.

A view from a different direction of the memorial.

Arthur's name is engraved on this portion of the wall.

Inside the chapel at the memorial.

Our gunship crew during a rest period.
Note the rockets to the left of photo.

Taking a picture of someone taking a picture.
Gunship in the background.

This pretty well wraps up two years in RVN. The next segment begins with a return to the States and going to work for the Iowa Army National Guard at the Army Aviation Support Facility in Waterloo, Iowa.

Our helicopter parking area and hangar.

My office in Waterloo with the National Guard.

Dad and Stanley playing chess.

An outpost of good guys in RVN.

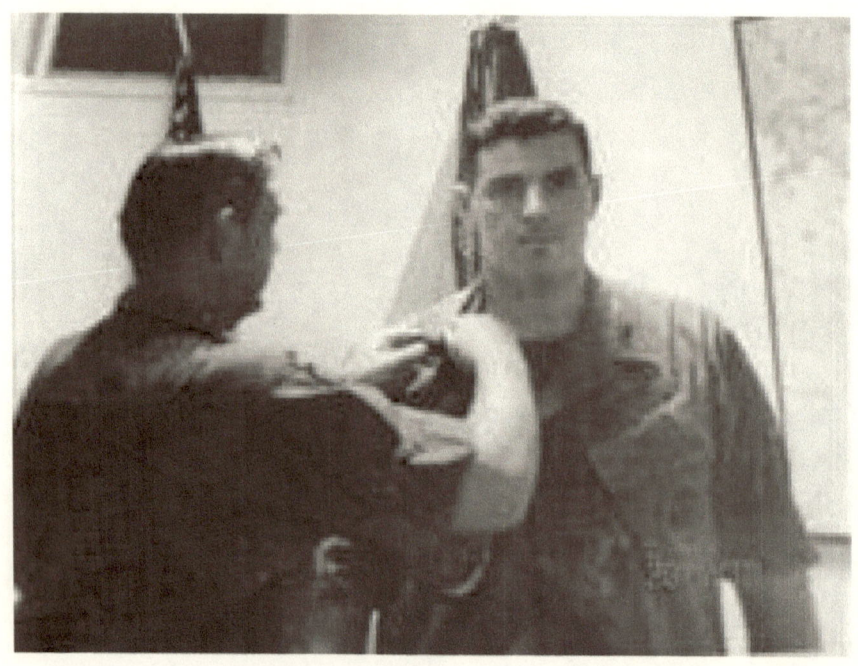
Receiving promotion to captain in RVN.

Jim Garner at our base in Ban Me Thuot on right.

Landing in LZ having green smoke.

Myself as a warrant officer.

Having landed in that LZ, off-loading supplies.

Myself as an officer first lieutenant.

In RVN, as a WO1 on my first tour.

In the office at Waterloo with the NG.

Receiving a medal from the general of Hunter AAF in Savannah, Georgia.

Driving an army jeep.

I had a few leftover photos from RVN that were on a different roll, and I wanted to get them in, so the last few pages have been mixed between Iowa and RVN.

Now that I arrived back home for good, I went to work applying for a position in the Iowa Army National Guard in Waterloo, Iowa. Iowa had not hired any new flight instructors for some time, and I and another ex-army IP were bidding on the same job. That was my first visit with Ed Sidler and Lynn Roskam. They were on the reviewing board, and I got selected. It was a full-time civil service technician position. I moved to Waterloo and began the new job. I still had my proficiency in flying to demonstrate, and I think Ed Sidler gave me that flight test. Then came all the paperwork for the position—government job, you know. That was done, and off to the races I went. I was still an army captain and had not learned the ropes with the National Guard. It did not take long, and I found out that I needed to adjust my ego a bunch.

I quickly adjusted to the environment. Made friends with most of the troop and was happy I had gotten the position.

National Guard was one weekend a month and two weeks in the summer. Of course, you had to add in twenty-four flight training drills then a few more days for whatever, and I ended up with about one or two weekends a month free. There was a winter camp for one year. It was on learning how to live out in the woods in the winter and doing some downhill and cross-country skiing. I worked hard at my job, and when a facility commander position opened, I was ready to apply. I applied and got selected for the position. It was in Davenport, Iowa, and a change of types of helicopters also. I took that job in 1978.

In 1980, I was looking for advancement, and I found it at Fort Rucker, Alabama. It was a competitive civil service position with chance for advancement. Off to Alabama I went. I will talk about Fort Rucker later, but now, let's talk about the Iowa National Guard.

One of our troop-carrying helicopters in RVN.
Note I am wearing my chicken-plate armor.

Sitting in my room at my desk. Had a little food, in case I came back late from a mission.

Working in my flight suit. I was about
185 lbs when I was in Vietnam.

One of the last photos I had taken for military records.
Note my medals on left chest and long sideburns.

Twenty-five years of government service.

Yearly review of my performance.

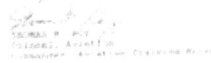

There are several of these certificates.

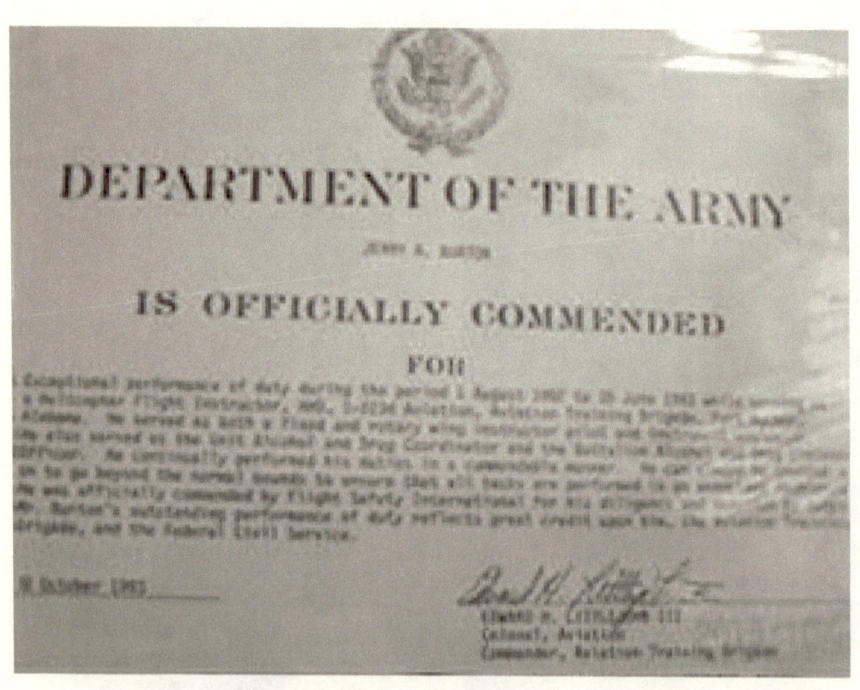

More "attaboys." Worked hard and the military showed their appreciation. Some came with a yearly bonus.

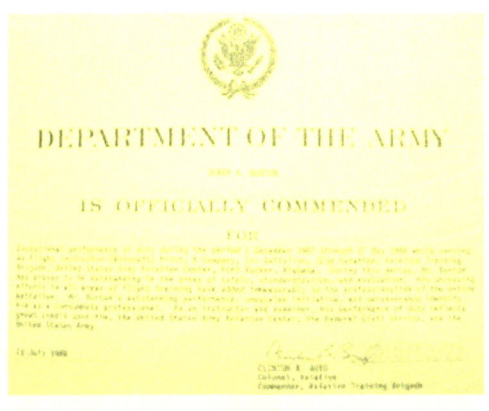

Received a promotion to GS-13 in 1983.
That was my highest pay grade at Fort Rucker.

I was at the flight controls of this Lear Jet
during my training on that airplane.

On one training flight, I flew from Grand Rapids, Michigan, to Waterloo, Iowa, and picked up Jeremy and Stephanie and took them back with me. Jeremy is at the front of the jet. It was a forty-two-minute flight. I received my Airline Transport Pilot rating and a Type rating in the Lear Jet. I parked it in front of the National Guard hangar in Waterloo.

This was my graduation certificate I received when
I passed my check ride with the FAA.

This was in front of the hangar back in Grand Rapids, Michigan. I received a total of eleven hours in the Lear, which included my 2-hour check ride. Never flew it again. I trained in it under the GI Bill. It cost $1,000.00 an hour to operate it and the GI bill paid 80 percent of the cost.

I received this certificate for the active duty service I completed.

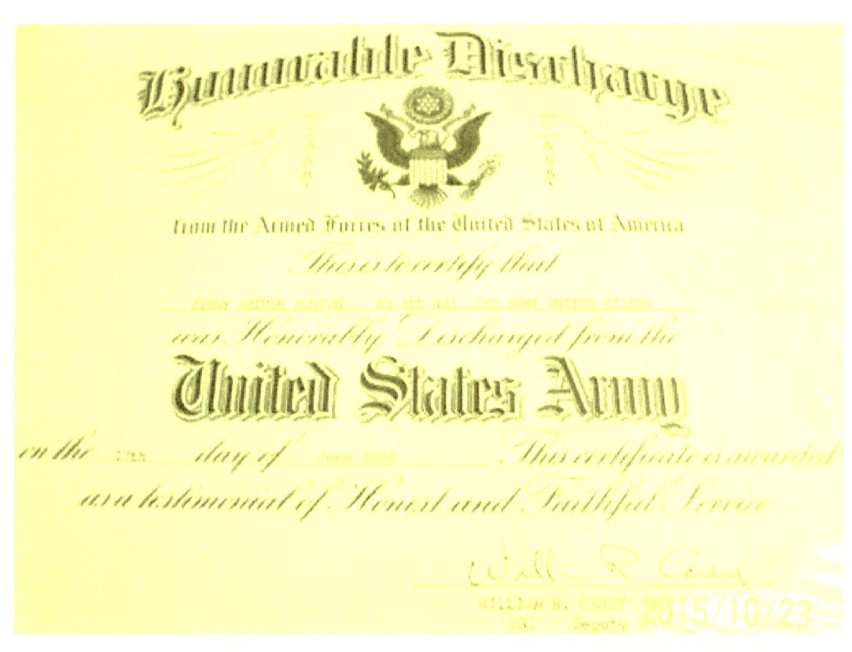

I received this one when I went between warrant
officer and commissioned service.

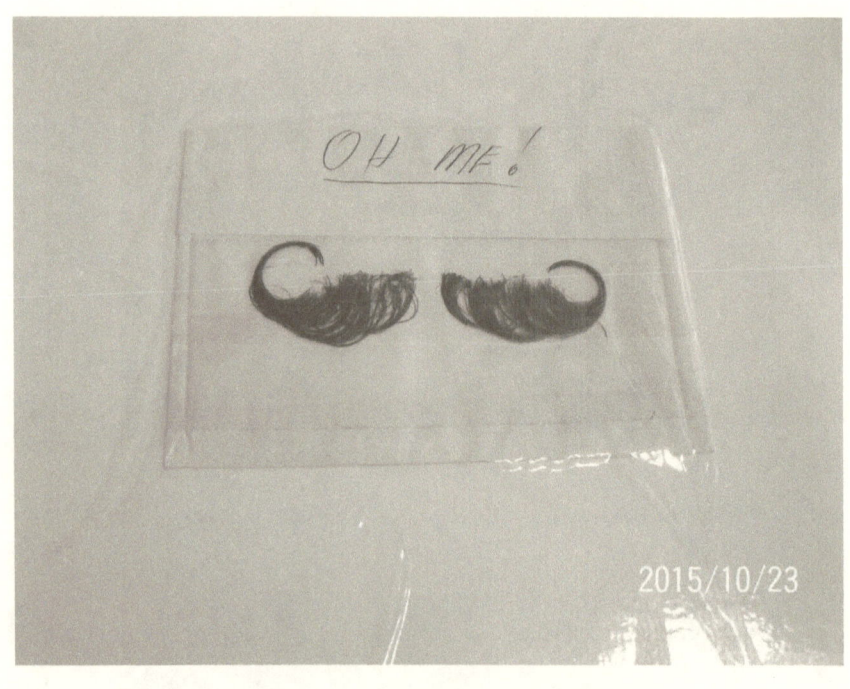

I cut my stache off before I came back from RVN. But kept it for the memories.

Got this from a safety school in Arizona.

Another school in Arizona.
The last school I went to in Arizona.

Vietnam Helicopter Pilots Association

devoted to the helicopter pilots who served their country in Southeast Asia during the Vietnam era, herein you know that

Jerry A Burton

has been granted all privileges in accordance with the Constitution and By-Laws of this organization

as a General Member

3782
Member Number

My membership in the VHPA.

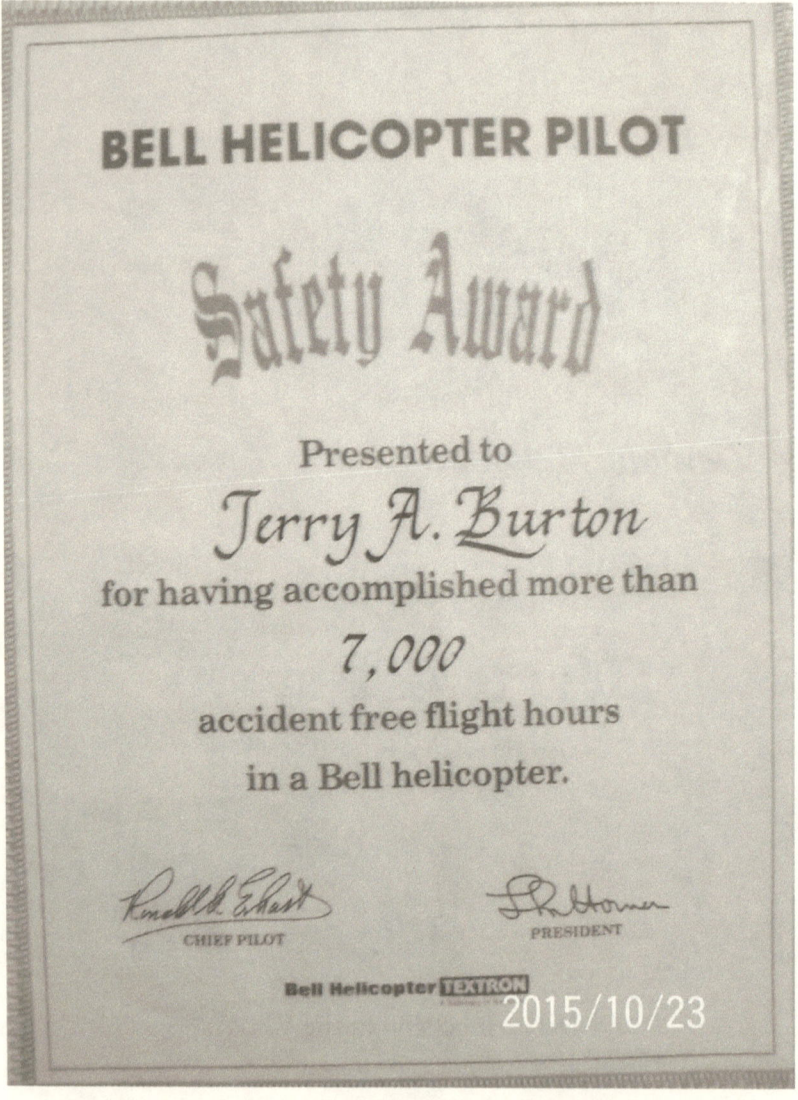

Received from Bell Helicopter for over 7,000 hours of helicopter hours in a Bell product.

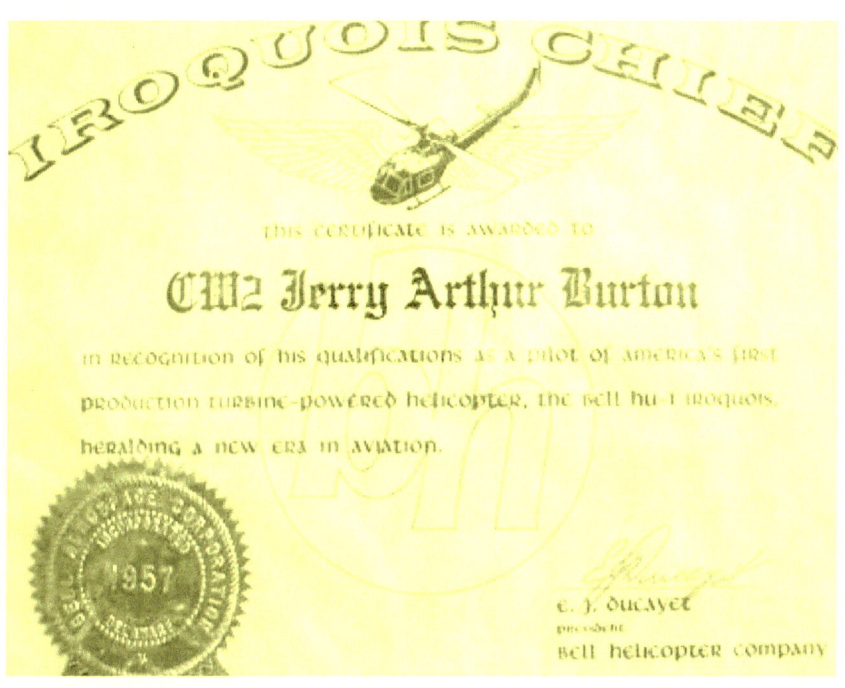

Another award from Bell Helicopter.

DEPARTMENT OF TRANSPORTATION
FEDERAL AVIATION ADMINISTRATION

Certificate of Training

JERRY A. BURTON

has satisfactorily completed a TWENTY hour course

PILOT EXAMINER STANDARDIZATION

given at LINCOLN, NEBRASKA

Dated this TWENTY FIRST day of JUNE 19 79

GAT STANDARDS NATIONAL FIELD OFFICE
EXAMINER STANDARDIZATION SECTION

GENERAL AVIATION DISTRICT OFFICE
LINCOLN, NEBRASKA

I was a designated pilot examiner for the FAA over several years and attended training course each year. My last designation in Alabama included both airplanes and helicopters. I was authorized to administer flight examinations in both through APT and Initial Flight Instructor.

Another FAA examiners course that I attended.

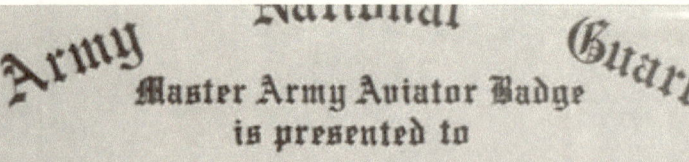

Here, I received my highest aviator badge,
the master army aviator badge.

A leadership course I attended at Camp Dodge, Iowa.

Attaboy for not having an accident while training initial entry students.

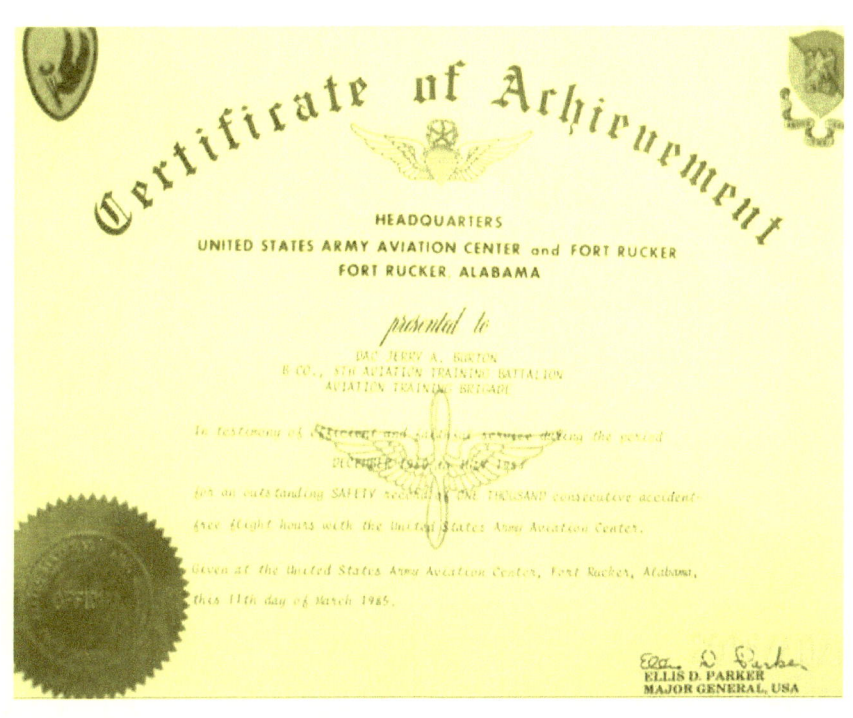

Certificate I received after finishing the instrument flight examiners training.

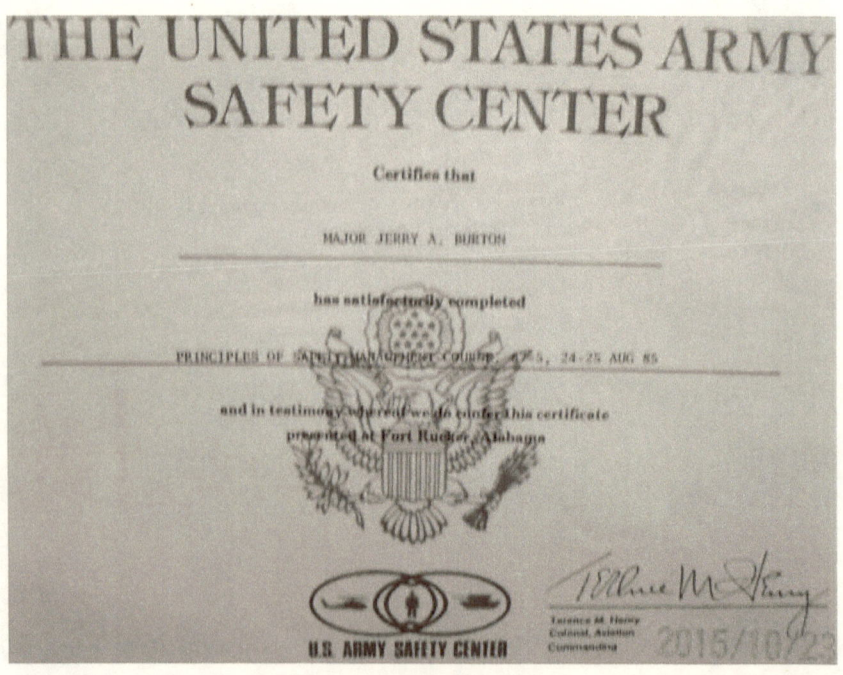

A short safety course.

DEPARTMENT OF THE ARMY
CERTIFICATE OF TRAINING

This is to certify that

JERRY A. BURTON

has successfully completed

C-12 AVIATOR QUALIFICATION COURSE, CLASS 90-13
6 Aug 90 - 17 Aug 90

Given at Fort Rucker, Alabama

MALVIN L. HANDY
COLONEL, AVIATION
DEPUTY ASSISTANT COMMANDANT

I completed the C-12 qualification course in 1990.
I later instructed in this training course.

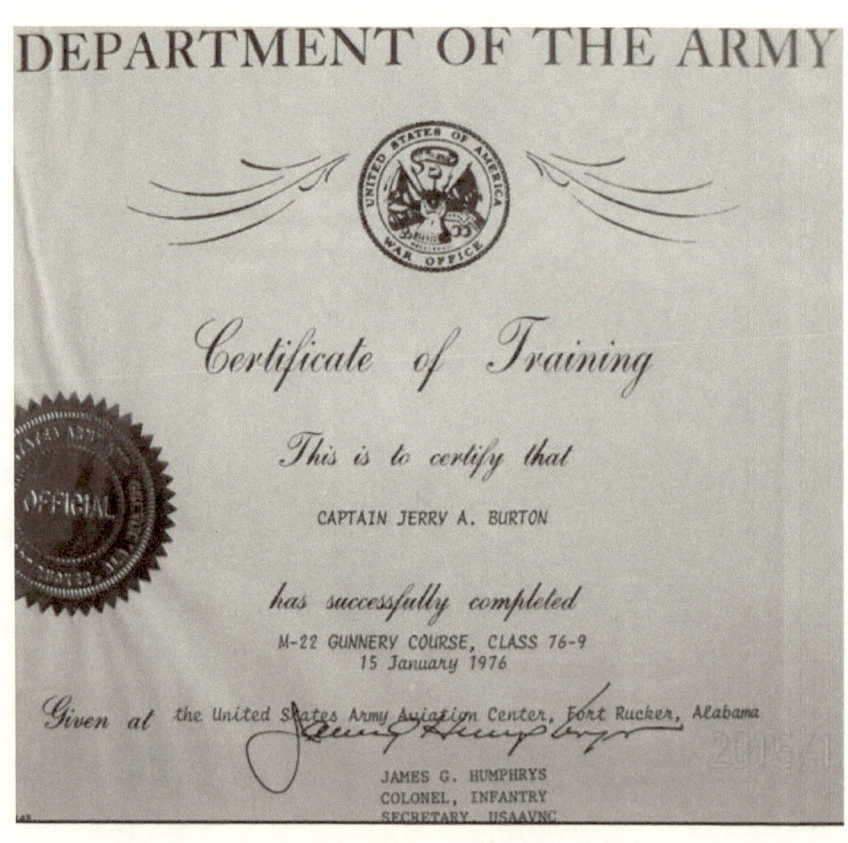

A gunnery course I attended.
This system was mounted on the gunships in Iowa Guard.

A safety course I attended for the Alabama National Guard.

Another safety course I attended. You can see by now that I went to school a lot.

Alabama National Guard.

Training I took while working at Fort Rucker.

More training in the Alabama Guard.

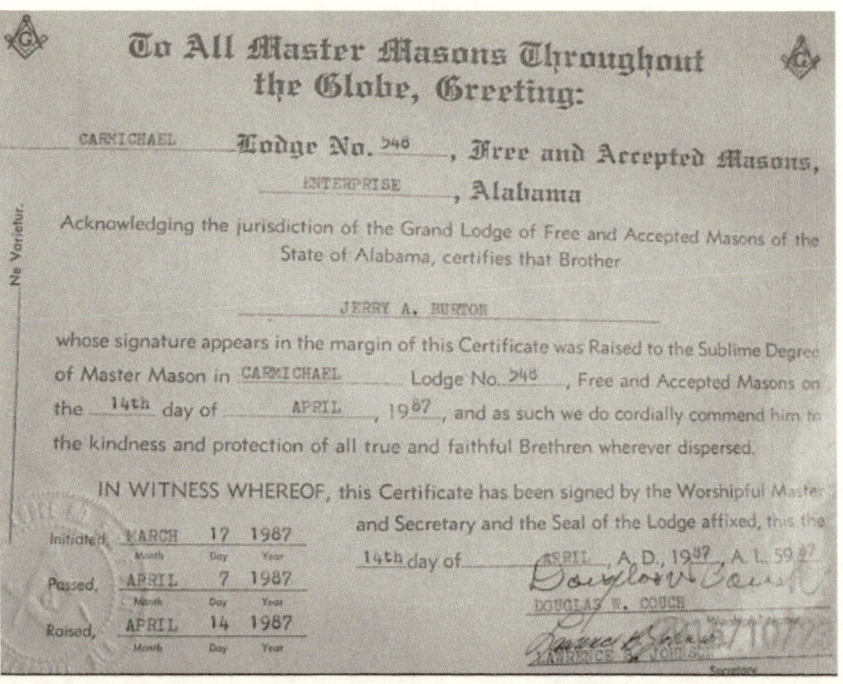

I joined the Masonic group and have been active in some capacity since. A very good group of men teaching biblical principles and brotherly fellowship.

I am a lifetime member of the first lodge of Masons that I joined.

A training course I attended while in the Civil Air Patrol.

Makes me feel old.

I am fourth from the left on the first row. Not much here, but it is me on my graduation from primary helicopter training in Fort Wolters, Texas. Nothing left of the base now, but it was near Mineral Wells, Texas. That would be about 40 miles west of Fort Worth.

This was the graduation class of safety officers.
I am in the first row, kneeling on the far right.

As I look back on my life in aviation, I am proud of the accomplishments that I have made and the flying that I have done. It started in 1964 and ended in 2002, thirty-eight years of being around airplanes and helicopters that have so many moving parts, which are there to make the airship fly. And if any of those parts quit while you're using it, the results could be bad. I have flown over 14,000 flight hours and was involved in only one accident—the one in Vietnam where I rolled down the hill. I was not at the controls, but what a ride it was. And I came out alive. Thank you, God.

There were some close calls, which we used to call hours and hours of boredom sprinkled with a few seconds of stark terror. Like any other career, I remember the good times and the not-so-good times. Not very many bad times. When the military was in bad times, it made your work harder; but that is part of life. No one said it was going to be easy all the time.

I do not miss the flying, but I do miss the pilots that I flew with during my career. One of the neatest things that I enjoyed was when I was at Fort Rucker—walking through the PX or in the classroom or on the flight line—and someone would come up to me and call me by name and tell me where we had met, and it was usually while flying some machine in training or on an evaluation flight. Sometimes I would remember the face but hardly ever remember the name. I find, at my age now, it is harder to remember new names. Usually takes me three or more times to remember a new name. Oh well, that is part of the aging process, they tell me. I have my share of those illnesses and ailments, like they say. If I had known that old age was going to be this bad, I would have taken better care of my body when I was young.

In my flying experience, I have flown a Lear Jet to 41,000 feet. The flight instructor asked me if I wanted the autopilot on, and I said no. When I am paying $1,000 an hour to fly this thing, I want to get every minute that I could hand flying.

I have flown a helicopter at a ridiculous high altitude and then flown them two or three feet above the South China Sea. Flown below the treetops to avoid hostile gunfire. I have lifted another helicopter out of a swampy area after it had an engine failure at Camp Ripley, Minnesota. I have been in the backseat of an OH-58A when the two pilots flying entered a cloud bank and had to turn around to get out of it. I was flying over the South China Sea in tight formation on the right side of another helicopter when the main rotor blades of both helicopters struck each other. We did not know until we landed how close to death we had come. The very tips of the main rotor blades had made contact with each other and had to be replaced before the aircraft could be flown again. Like I said before, it's hours and hours of boredom streaked by a few seconds of stark terror.

While I was stationed at Fort Rucker, I received a mission to Yuma, Arizona, in a U-21A airplane; and on the way out, we had the opportunity to fly over the Grand Canyon. It was one of the most beautiful sights I have ever seen. It's pretty from the ground but unbelievable from the air. Sedona, Arizona, is another wonderful place to fly into and out of. The scenery is overwhelming.

In the summer of 2015, I was invited to a Vietnam Veterans Welcome Home Weekend in Forest City, Iowa. It was a wonderful experience—all those veterans like me getting together to celebrate returning home after the war. It was a little late (like forty-seven years) but greatly appreciated by all who attended. They had helicopter rides and a flight demonstration of several different aircraft. The movable Vietnam Memorial Wall was there also. It was a very moving experience for me—quite emotional and lots of memories. It made me feel like I was appreciated for what I had done over there in RVN.

The second significant emotional experience of 2015 was being selected to go on an Honor Flight to Washington, DC, and visit all the war memorials. There was more to the trip than I knew about. The trip was one day long, and what an exciting time. I had a guardian to help me get around the memorials and on and off the bus. We had a police escort all over the city from our arrival at the airport until we returned for our flight home.

The flight home and our arrival at the Cedar Rapids, Iowa, airport was a big surprise. On the flight home, the group that sponsored the trip surprised me with letters that had been written by my family, welcoming me home. Then when we departed the airplane, they had a band playing for us, and our families were there to welcome us home. *Wow!* What an emotional experience. It made me feel so special. I have included several photos of both trips.

At the War Memorial looking toward the Lincoln.

Eric and me at the Lincoln.

My guardian and his wife.

Terry Nelson, a good friend killed in an accident.

Vietnam wall. Awesome.

Eric and I at Korean War Memorial.

A guard at the Tomb of the Unknown Soldier.

Laying wreath at a tomb and changing of the guard at the Tomb of the Unknown Soldier.

Raising the flag at Iwo Jima Memorial.

In Forest City, Iowa, at the Welcome Veterans Weekend. I had a golf cart to get around.

All veterans received one of these medals.

A Cobra helicopter (AH-1) escorts the moving
Vietnam wall along its trip to our camp.

A big truck and several hundred motorcycles escort the moving wall along its route.

The crowd gathered when the wall entered the landing zone.

A Mohawk (OV-1) puts on a demonstration flight at the airport.

The helicopters gave rides for those that wanted them.
I decided not to, would rather fly the things.

The Cobra puts on a flying demonstration.
That's a 20mm gun just below the nose.

Buon Me Thuot and Can Tho are the two locations we were based at, although we flew over most of South Vietnam, south of Quang Tri. Just north of there was where the border between north and south was located, and it was guarded by the North Vietnam troops. A bad place to go for a picnic. I spent a lot of time in Nha Trang and Vung Tau, doing training and missions.

Diary entry.

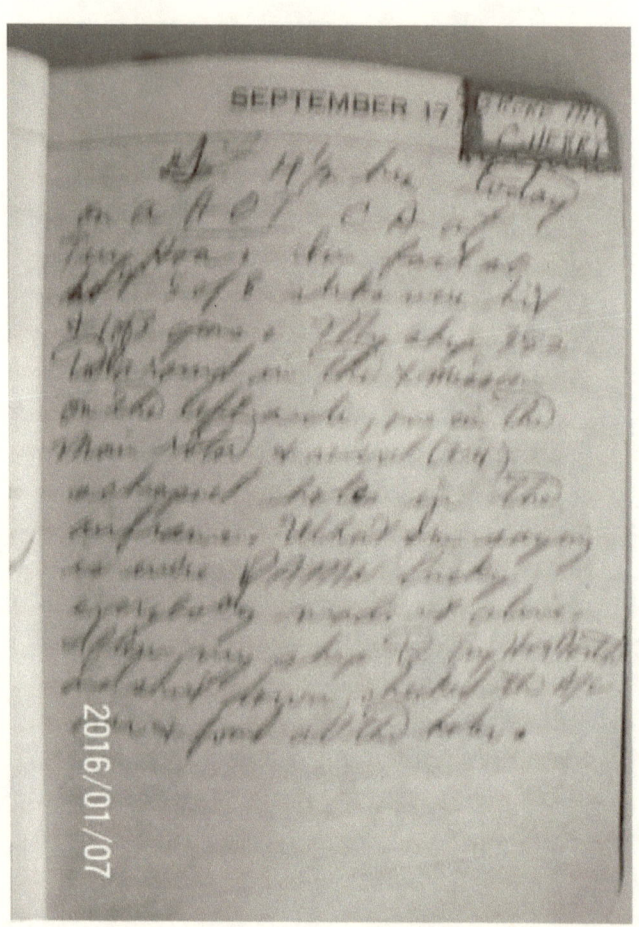

My aircraft received several enemy bullets but was not shot down.

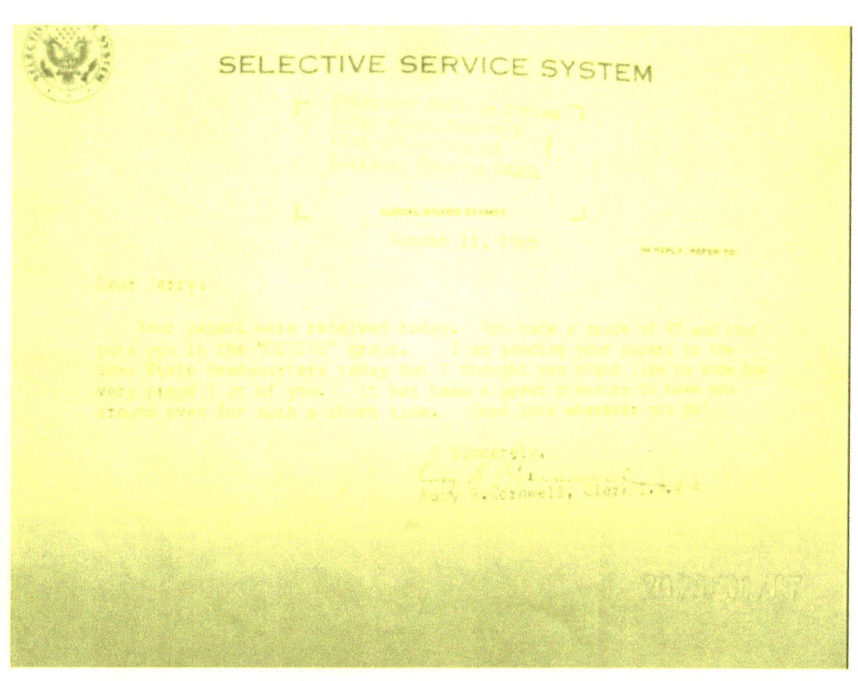

The grade I received on this examination was 97, which put me in the genius group.

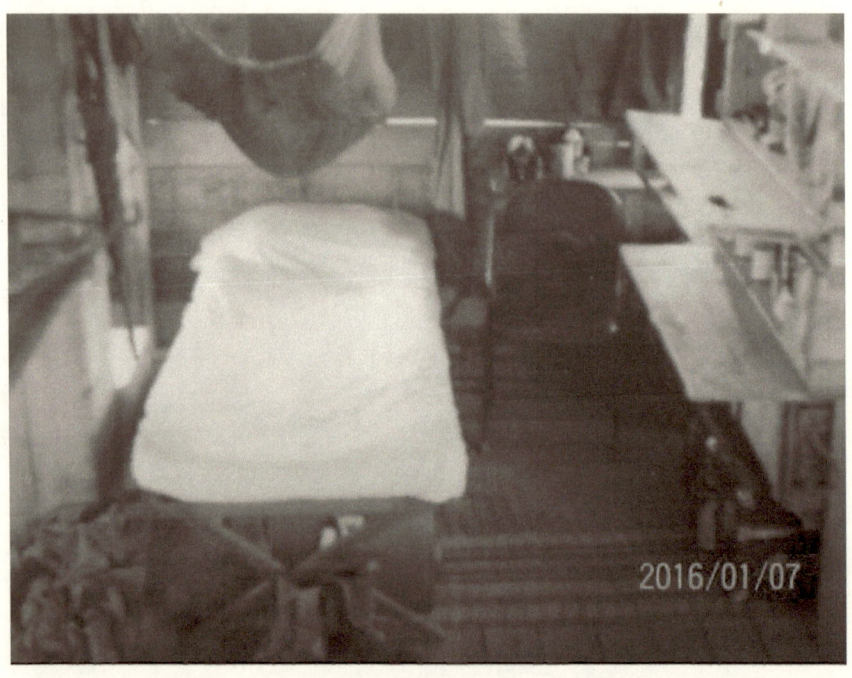

This was my room in 1967. Notice the bug net over the bed and my desk on the right.

I received this plaque when I went on the Honor Flight to DC and viewed the war memorials.

The medal I received at Operation LZ
at Forest City, Iowa, in 2015.

WAR TROPHY REGISTRATION/AUTHORIZATION		
INSTRUCTIONS: This form will be prepared for all types of war trophies. Original to owner; 1 copy with trophy; 1 copy retained by issuing command. If war trophy is a firearm, DD Form 603 will also be prepared.		
Theater and inclusive period of service in overseas command
Republic of Viet Nam 31 May, 70 to 31 May, 71		
Name of Owner (Last, First, MI)
BURTON, JERRY A	Service Number	Grade/Rank
CPT 03
Organization
HHT 7/1 AIR CAV APO 96357	Permanent Home Address
Box 495, Alden, Iowa, 50006	
DESCRIPTION OF WAR TROPHY		
Describe Item (If firearm, indicate make, type - rifle/pistol
MAUSER RIFLE, MODEL 98, 7.92 mm		
Serial Number or Identifying Mark (if firearm, include country of manufacture)
9045 Lawrence C Kreps, Jr
GERMANY		
Date
20 Feb, 71	Typed Name, Grade, Org of Authenticating Officer
LAWRENCE C KREPS, JR, SFC, USA, CMEC	
Station
APO SF 96307	Signature
Lawrence C Kreps Jr.	
DD Form 603-1, 1 Jul 65		

This was how I registered one of the two war trophies that I brought home. It took about four months to do the paperwork.

```
                WAR TROPHY REGISTRATION/AUTHORIZATION
INSTRUCTIONS: This form will be prepared for all types of war trophies. Original
to owner; 1 copy with trophy; 1 copy retained by issuing command. If war trophy
is a firearm, DD Form 603 will also be prepared.
Theater and inclusive  period of service in overseas command
Republic of Viet Nam       31 May, 70   to   31 May, 71
Name of Owner (Last, First, MI)        Service Number      Grade/Rank

BURTON, JERRY A                                            CPT O3
Organization                           Permanent Home Address

  HHT 7/1 AIR CAV  APO 96357             Box 495, Alden, Iowa, 50006
                       DESCRIPTION OF WAR TROPHY
Describe Item (If firearm, indicate make, type - rifle/pistol

  CHICOM CARBINE, TYPE 56, 7.62 mm, w/ Bayonet
Serial Number or Identifying Mark (if firearm, include country of manufacture)

  13063946  COMMUNIST CHINA
Date                    Typed Name, Grade, Org of Authenticating Officer

  20 Feb, 71              LAWRENCE C KREPS, JR, SFC, USA, CMEC
Station                 Signature
  APO SF 96307             Lawrence C Kreps, Jr
DD Form 603-1, 1 Jul 65
```

This is the other weapon, a Chicom rifle I brought home. This one was new, never fired, and it is on display at the National Guard Gold Star Museum at Camp Dodge, Iowa.

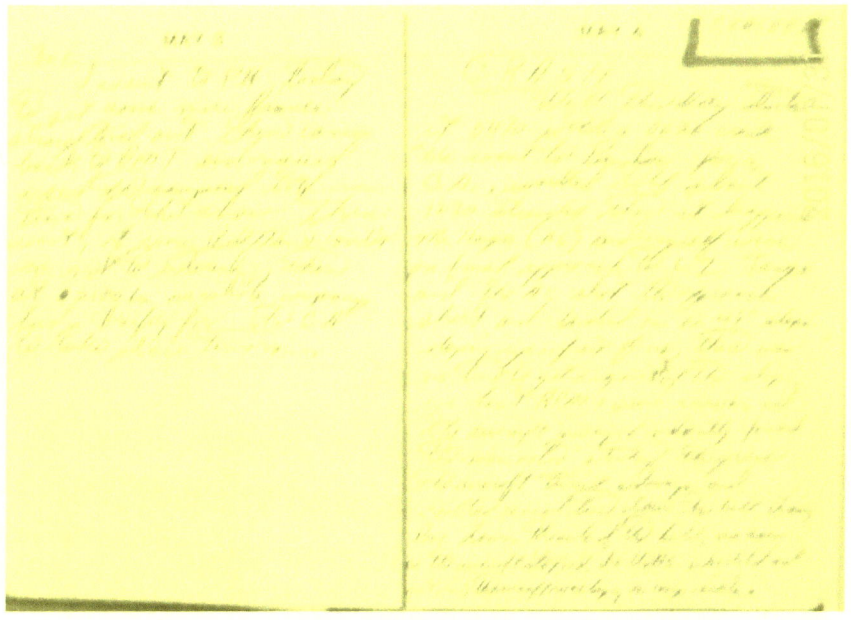

An entry in my diary about the only day in my life that I was in a helicopter that crashed. It was a mess, but the crew only received bumps and bruises. Killed some passengers though.

A certificate awarded to me for completing a course of instruction with the Civil Air Patrol. I was a member for three to four years. They had a Cessna 172 that I flew for search and rescue. I also took it on a proficiency flight to Dallas, Texas, to visit my friend from basic training. Judy, my wife, was also a member of the CAP.

Here Judy and I are enjoying some time off from Simcom in Port St. John visiting my Brother Bud and his wife Mary. It was always enjoyable to get away from work and visit family. We spent many a weekend with them. Playing cards was their entertainment and we let them win most of the time.
I was blessed with five children. Starting at the oldest to youngest they are Brian, Lora, Bryan, Stephanie and Jeremy. All but Brian reside in Alabama.

Top photo: While I was working for Simcom in Arizona I purchased this little red convertible and enjoyed driving it to work most ever day. Even in the winter the temperature was not that bad and it does not rain very often in Arizona.

Bottom photo: We occasionally flew customer's aircraft, here I am in Right seat of a King Air on a trip somewhere. Again in Arizona the weather was nice most of the time.

Top photo: Here my photo was taken while retired in my favorite jacket. A local business was taking veterans pictures and they gave me a copy. I had been retired a couple years at this point.

Bottom photo: This park was dedicated to our family name in the small town of Alden Iowa. The story goes that my father owned this entire block of town and when he passed away it was divided among the four sons. We kept it many years until a city group bought the entire section and are developing it into a sports complex with our family name on it. Our whole family was pretty happy about that.

Top photo: This picture shows Dad with his four sons. I am on the far left then Bud, Dad Floyd and Stanley. It was taken on Dads last farm in front of the house. Mother passed away when I was about 5 years old. There was 13 years between me and my next oldest brother, now you figure that one out.

Bottom photo: Here I was receiving my commission as a Warrant Officer and Dad and my brother Bud were pining on my WO1 bars on my shoulders. It was at Fort Wolters Texas Army base.

Top: This is my group of American Legion members. I am on the top row second from the right. We have a good group of men and women, it's a small legion post but we get a lot of work done.

Bottom: Here we are at the Fourth of July parade and I am driving the Legion machine. We were in the parade every year. The Lions club put on the parade and one year we were selected as the Grand Marshals for the parade. It was quite an honor and we were very humble.

HEADQUARTERS 2D BATTALION
2D TRAINING REGIMENT, BASIC
UNITED STATES ARMY TRAINING CENTER
Fort Leonard Wood, Missouri 65475

6 December 1965

DISTINGUISHED TRAINEE AWARD

SCORE "90"

PRIVATE JERRY A. BURTON, RA17731542

COMPANY "C"

is cited for achieving the above score that exceeds the mark of EIGHTY-FIVE out of ONE HUNDRED POINTS, which has been established as the standard of distinction in the BASIC TRAINING PROFICIENCY TEST . . . .

RICHARD J. MCFERRIN
Captain, Infantry
Company Commander

JOE W. FINLEY
Lt Col, Infantry
Battalion Commander

This was my basic training award that I received for my proficiency test. Did pretty good for an ole farm boy.

155th ASSAULT HELICOPTER COMPANY
FALCONS

This certifies that

Did successfully progress through the fledgling state to become a member of the famous FALCON FIGHTER PILOTS, U.S. Army Air Corps, and privileged to wear the Distinctive emblem and cap of the Fighting Flying Falcons . . .
. . . and during the period _____ to _____ provided unrelenting direct air support, in combat, to fellow Stagecoachers and other military and civil units throughout South Vietnam.
This certificate is awarded in appreciation of this member's unselfish dedication toward the achievement of overall unit success.
Given this date _____, at Ban Me Thuot, Republic of South Vietnam.

This was my first tour in RVN and the time I spent with the gun platoon called the Falcons. Was more safe than flying the slicks that landed into the hot LZ. Of course more damage was done with the gun ship also. We had 7.62 mini guns, 2.75 inch rockets and 40 mm grenade launchers

155th ASSAULT HELICOPTER COMPANY
STAGECOACHERS

This certifies that

JERRY A. BURTON	WO1	W3155431
Name	Rank	Serial Number

Was initiated on **7 MARCH 1967** and became a member of the FIGHTING STAGE-COACHERS, privileged to wear the distinctive Stagecoach Patch, with authority to take part in any and all assigned Stagecoach missions . . . .

. . . . and during the period **7 MARCH 1967** to **29 FEBRUARY 68** unselfishly carried out assigned tasks throughout South Vietnam, and did many times endure the hardships of weather and terrain, critical time schedules, and enemy action.

This certificate is awarded in appreciation of this member's commendable services. Given this date **29 FEBRUARY 68**, at Ban Me Thuot, Republic of South Vietnam.

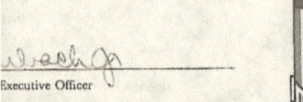

Executive Officer   Commanding Officer

This was my first tour when I flew troop carrying helicopters. They were a good group of guys and some did not go home alive. In this platoon we took troops from a base out to fight the bad guys. Lots of flying hours, about 1000 hours each year in RVN.

Certificate of Achievement

Awarded By The Commanding General Of The United States
Army Aviation Center In Behalf Of Army Aviation To:

JERRY A. BURTON

For Writing The Article:

"ENGINE FAILURE IMC WITH LOW CEILINGS"

Which Was Selected For Publication In

APRIL 1988

ELLIS D. PARKER
Major General, U.S. Army
Commanding Officer

m 500, 1 Oct 79

This certificate was awarded to me when I wrote an article about an engine failure while I was teaching with the RWIFEC, rotary wing instrument flight examiners course. I was in the back jump seat with two National Guard students flying up front. We were half way between Montgomery AI and Fort Rucker AL. When with no notice the engine failed. We all three turned into a fine tuned crew with the two up front doing the flying and I making the May Day call. You can read the article later on but things went our way and with the help of the Man above we landed in a field with no damage or injury.

HEADQUARTERS
1ST AVIATION BRIGADE
APO San Francisco 96384

GENERAL ORDERS   "NGUY HIEM"   12 August 1968
NUMBER   5533

AWARD OF THE AIR MEDAL FOR HEROISM

1. TC 320. The following AWARD is announced.

BURTON, JERRY A. ███████ SSAN: ███████ WARRANT OFFICER W1
United States Army, 155th Aslt Hel Co, APO 96297
Awarded: Air Medal with "V" Device
Date action: 30 January 1968
Theater: Republic of Vietnam
Reason: For heroism while engaged in aerial flight in connection with military operations against a hostile force: Warrant Officer Burton distinguished himself by exceptionally valorous actions during the rescue of the crew of a downed helicopter gunship near Ban Me Thuot. He volunteered his services as pilot to make up a crew to go to the rescue, conducted a quick pre-flight inspection and selected one of the least severely damaged ships for the mission. As the gunship arrived at the crash scene, it received intense fire. He immediately returned the fire and located the downed crew in a small clearing. He wisely dropped a smoke grenade marking the landing zone for a dustoff pick-up and laid down a heavy concentration of fire on the enemy positions, thus making a successful rescue possible. His actions were in keeping with the highest traditions of the military service and reflect great credit upon himself, his unit, and the United States Army.
Authority: By direction of the President under the provisions of Executive Order 9158, 11 May 1942, as amended by Executive Order 9242-A, 11 September 1942 and United States Army Vietnam Message 16695 dated 1 July 1966.

FOR THE COMMANDER:

OFFICIAL: HERB D. PRATHER
                                         COL, INF
                                         Chief of Staff

LEE S. PETERSON
1LT, AGC
Asst Adjutant General

DISTRIBUTION: SPECIAL DISTRIBUTION:
25 AVBA-AG-AD   1 TAGO ATTN: AGPP-O
 1 Record Copy   1 DIR OPD OPO WD
 1 Reference Copy
 1 USARV ATTN: AVHAG-PD
 2 CINCUSARPAC ATTN: GPOP-MH
 1 CINCUSARPAC ATTN: AG-DP
 1 IO

This order was awarded to me for a mission I went on to rescue a crew that had been shot down just south of Ban Me Tout Army Base.

Army Aviation Broken Wing Award

presented to

MR. JERRY A. BURTON

who

while performing flight duty on

22 SEPTEMBER 1993

displayed extraordinary skill, judgment, and technique during an in-flight emergency. In spite of extreme circumstances which might have led to catastrophic results, a successful landing was achieved through application of the highest degree of proficiency and discretion.

R. DENNIS KERR
Brigadier General
Director of Army Safety

I received the Army's Broken Wing award when I was flying at Fort Rucker and had a in-flight emergency with a safe landing and no injury.

This was me receiving the Broken Wing award.

This is the first Officer leadership Course that was conducted in the Iowa Army National Guard. I am in front center and was the class leader for the course.

This was a summer camp with the Iowa Army National Guard at Camp Ripley Mn. It was a year that a lot of the troops rode their motorcycles to summer camp. LTC Gamer was our Squadron commander in the center and Major Edward Sidler is just to the left of him.

JOSEPH B. FLATT
BRIGADIER GENERAL

Commander Of Troops
Iowa Army National Guard
Red Horse Armory
Des Moines, Iowa 50310

25 June 1971

SUBJECT: Appointment

CPT Jerry A. Burton
P. O. Box 495
Alden, Iowa 50006

1. I am very pleased to note your appointment as an officer in the Iowa Army National Guard and as a reserve officer of the Army. You may be justly proud that the State and Nation have placed such trust and confidence in your abilities.

2. As Commander of Troops, I welcome you to the ranks of a corps of professional officers. I further charge you to accept your new responsibilities with all of the motivation and dedication that earned you your appointment.

JOSEPH B. FLATT
BG, Iowa ARNG
Commander of Troops

My appointment letter into the Iowa Army National Guard .

FlightSafety International

Certifies that

JERRY A. BURTON

has satisfactorily completed a course of

Simulator Instructor Training in the C-12 (BE-200)

11th day of November 19 86

Britt Hoskins, MANAGER

afety device in any aircraft is a well trained pilot...

This is my completion certificate from Flight Safety upon completing the C-12 (king air 200) course. I worked full and part time for this company while at Fort Rucker AI.

DEPARTMENT OF TRANSPORTATION
FEDERAL AVIATION ADMINISTRATION

Certificate of Training

JERRY A. BURTON

has satisfactorily completed a TWENTY hour course

PILOT EXAMINER STANDARDIZATION

given at LINCOLN, NEBRASKA

Dated this TWENTY FIRST day of JUNE 19 79

FLIGHT STANDARDS NATIONAL FIELD OFFICE
EXAMINER STANDARDIZATION SECTION

GENERAL AVIATION DISTRICT O
LINCOLN, NEBRASKA

This one of the designated pilot examiner courses that I attended while I was doing that duty for the FAA.

Low Flight

Oh I have lifted vertically from the ground
And humbly joined the sky while wings swept round;
Forward I've flown, while closely hugging earth
Beneath the clouds, and done a hundred things you would not dare do:
Autoed, hoisted and beeped while challenging death.
Hovering there I've fought the shifting winds around
And forced my balking craft through fearful turbulent air
Down amongst the low awaiting fog -
I've stayed above the sea
Through skill - where never goat nor even C-130 flew.
And while with silent humble stance,
I've listened to the men who fly on high.
I've lowered my head and taken their abuse
And somewhere God looked at me and smiled.

This is the poem of Low Flight, one that was for helicopter pilots.

This is my high school picture. I got better with age.

Alcazar
TEMPLE
A. A. O. N. M. S.

To all True and Faithful Nobles
Know Ye that the Worthy Noble

Jerry Burton

Has been awarded this

Certificate of Service

In appreciation of his meritorious
and faithful service as

Director

for the year
1989

An award I received while in the Shrine temple in Montgomery AL.

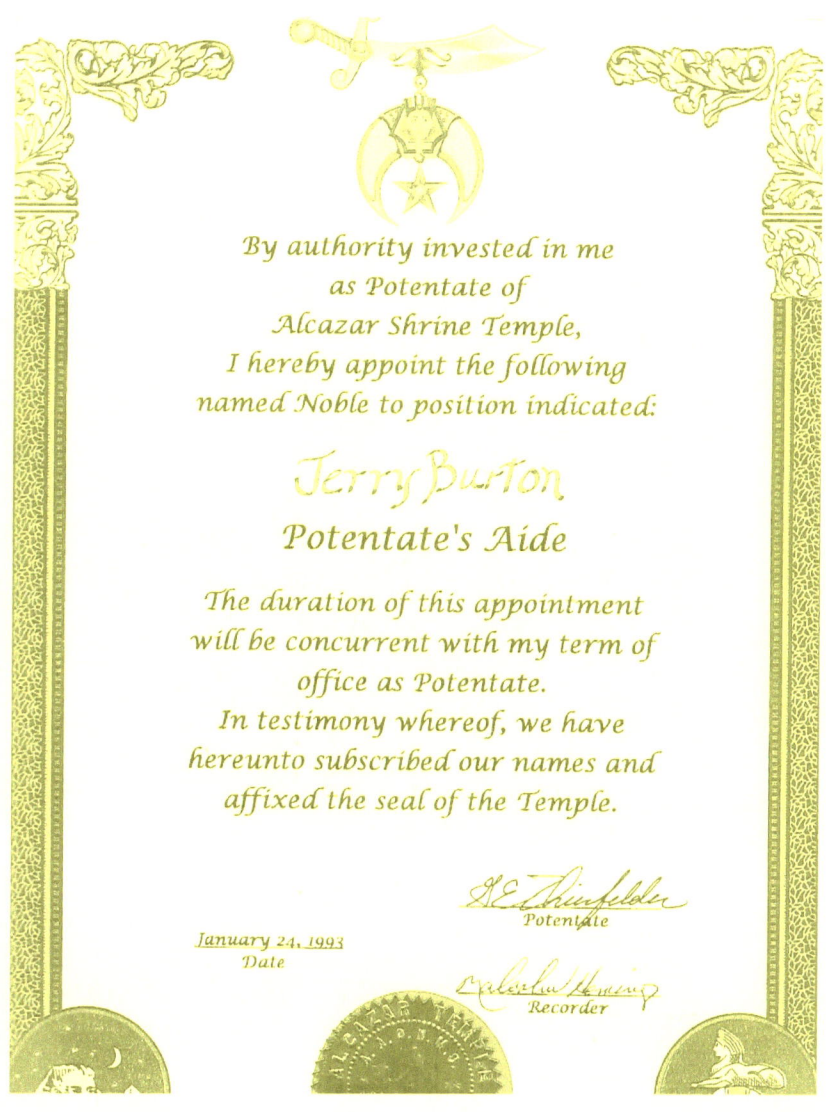

Another certificate I received while in the Shrine organization.